ANNIKA SORENSTAM

DISCOVER THE LIFE OF A SPORTS STAR II

David and Patricia Armentrout

Rourke
Publishing LLC
Vero Beach, Florida 32964

www.rourkepublishing.com

PHOTO CREDITS:
Cover, Page 19 ©Scott Halleran/Getty Images; Title, Page 6 ©Sven Nackstrand/AFP/Getty Images; Page 8 ©Pontus Lundahl/AFP/Getty Images; Page 7 ©Nick Wilson/Allsport; Page 10 ©David Cannon/Getty Images; Page 12 ©Paul Barker/AFP/Getty Images; Page 15 ©Steve Munday/Allsport; Page 4 ©Jeff Gross/Getty Images; Page 17 ©J.D. Cuban/Getty Images; Pages 5, 18, 21 ©Andy Lyons/Getty Images

Title page: *Swedish golf fans watch Annika Sorenstam consider her putt.*

Editor: Frank Sloan

Cover and interior design by Nicola Stratford

Library of Congress Cataloging-in-Publication Data

Armentrout, David, 1962-
  Annika Sorenstam / David and Patricia Armentrout.
     p. cm. — (Discover the life of a sports star II)
  Includes bibliographical references (p.   ) and index.
  ISBN 1-59515-130-3 (hardcover)
  1. Sorenstam, Annika, 1970---Juvenile literature. 2. Tennis players--United States--Biography--Juvenile literature. I. Armentrout, Patricia, 1960- II. Title. II. Series: Armentrout, David, 1962-   Discover the life of a sports star II.
  GV994.S67A76 2004
  796.352'092--dc22

                                                    2004007637

Printed in the USA

CG/CG

Table of Contents

Annika celebrates after making two shots below par on the ninth hole.

Annika Sorenstam

Annika Sorenstam is a world-class golfer. Her list of **tournament** victories and golfing awards could easily fill the pages of this book. Annika is already one of the greatest golfers of all time, and she may not have reached her peak yet.

Born: October 9, 1970
Birth Place: Stockholm,
   Sweden
LPGA Rookie Year: 1994
Inducted into Hall of Fame: 2003

Athletic Childhood

Growing up in Sweden, Annika and her younger sister Charlotta played all kinds of sports. During the long winters they skied and played indoor tennis and volleyball. In the summer they played soccer and badminton and spent as much time as possible outdoors. Eventually, Annika and Charlotta focused their athletic ability on tennis. In fact, both girls were ranked junior **amateur** tennis players in Sweden.

Annika plays on familiar turf in Stockholm, Sweden.

Annika with her sister Charlotta at the Women's World Cup of Golf in Malaysia

Annika's passion shows after sinking a putt during a match against Angela Stansford.

A New Passion

Annika gradually lost interest in tennis. At age 16, she put down her tennis racket for good. She told her parents she wanted to play golf. The more she played, the more she realized how much she loved the sport. To be a competitor, Annika would have to practice year round.

Golfing is a warm-weather sport and Sweden has wintry weather at least six months of the year. Always willing to do what it takes, Annika sometimes used an orange golf ball so she could play in the snow.

Annika's coach Henri Reis watches her technique during practice.

Coaching Counts

Annika credits two of her long-time coaches for much of her golfing success. Her first coach, Henri Reis, began teaching Annika when she was 16. Annika continues to meet with Reis several times a year to fine tune her skills. Annika has also benefited from a close relationship with Pia Nilsson. Nilsson, an accomplished Swedish golfer in her own right, has coached Annika for many years.

Annika tees off.

A Good Start

In 1990, Annika accepted a golf scholarship to the University of Arizona. Her success at the university was almost immediate. In her first year, she won numerous amateur titles and was the 1991 **NCAA** college player of the year. Her success helped lead the Arizona Wildcats to the NCAA championship. Annika was an NCAA All-American in 1991 and 1992.

Rookie of the Year

Annika turned **professional** in 1993, but didn't become a full-time member of the **LPGA** Tour until 1994. She did not win any LPGA tournaments that year, but tied for second place at the Women's British Open. Her friend Liselotte Neumann, also from Sweden, won the event. Annika played well enough her first year to win the LPGA Rolex Rookie of the Year award.

Annika practices in West Virginia during her first year as a pro.

Player of the Year

Annika didn't slow down in 1995. She got her first victory on the LPGA Tour at the U.S. Open. She also won the Heartland Classic and the Samsung World Championship of Women's Golf. She finished the year as the LPGA Rolex Player of the Year. Annika is the second player in history to win Rookie of the Year, followed by Player of the Year the following season.

Annika blasts a shot out of a sand trap and goes on to win the event.

Posing with her 2003 "Player of the Year" trophy

It's All about Winning

In 1996, Annika won the U.S. Open for the second straight year. She won six tournaments in 1997 and in 1998 surpassed the $3 million mark in career earnings. In 2001, she claimed an incredible eight tournament victories. The year 2002 was another good one for Annika. She became the second player in history to win 11 LPGA titles in one season. Annika won the LPGA Rolex Player of the Year award again in 1997, 1998, 2001, 2002, and 2003.

Annika signs autographs after the Sybase Big Apple Classic.

A World-Class Golfer

Annika was inducted into the World Golf Hall of Fame in 2003. But it was her appearance in the **PGA** Colonial tournament that made the biggest headlines. Why was this news? Women don't traditionally compete in the PGA. The last woman to do this had been Babe Didrikson in 1945.

Annika accepted the challenge with grace. She played well, but did not make it to the final rounds. However, she did show that women can be competitive against men in golf, and that she is one of the world's best golfers!

Walking with Dean Wilson, one of her playing partners, at the PGA Colonial

Dates to Remember

1970   Born in Stockholm, Sweden

1990   Accepts golf scholarship to the University of Arizona

1991   NCAA college player of the year

1994   Wins LPGA Rookie of the Year

1995   First LPGA victory at the U.S. Open

1995   Wins LPGA Rolex Player of the Year for the first time

2003   Plays in PGA Colonial

2003   Inducted into World Golf Hall of Fame

Glossary

amateur (AM uh tur) — someone who participates in a sport for pleasure rather than for money

LPGA (LPGA) — Ladies Professional Golf Association

NCAA National Collegiate Athletic Association — A group of colleges, universities, and other athletic groups who establish programs to govern and promote athletics

PGA — Professional Golfers Association

professional (pruh FESH un ul) — a paid instructor or athlete

tournament (TUR nuh muhnt) — an organized golf competition

Index

Further Reading

Ditchfield, Christin. *Golf.* Children's Press, 2003.
Gordon, John. *The Kids Book of Golf.* Kids Can Press, 2001.
Stenzel, Kellie. *The Women's Guide to Golf: A Handbook for Beginners.*
    Thomas Dunne Books, 2000.

Websites To Visit

www.lpga.com
www.learnaboutgolf.com

About The Authors

David and Patricia Armentrout have written many nonfiction books for young readers. They have had several books published for primary school reading. The Armentrouts live in Cincinnati, Ohio, with their two children.